GENERATION CRICKET

PLAYERS AND SKILLS

Clive Gifford

First published in 2015 by Wayland
Copyright © Wayland 2015

Wayland
338 Euston Road
London NW1 3BH

Wayland Australia
Level 17/207 Kent Street
Sydney, NSW 2000

Editor: Elizabeth Brent
Designer: Peter Clayman

Dewey number: 796.3'58-dc23

ISBN 978 0 7502 8300 7
eBook ISBN 978 0 7502 9299 3

Printed in China

10 9 8 7 6 5 4 3 2 1

Picture acknowledgements: Cover: © AFP/Getty images (main), © Scott Barbour/Getty images (bl), Gareth Copley/Getty images (bm), PAUL ELLIS/AFP/Getty images; p1: Getty images/Gareth Copley; p4: Getty images/Saeed Khan; p5: Getty images/Hamish Blair (t), Getty images/Hagen Hopkins; p6–7: Getty images/Matthew Lewis-iDi; p8: Getty images/ishara S. Kodikara/AFP; p9: © Stefan Chabluk (l); © Getty images/Dorling Kindersley (r); p10: © Getty images/Matt King (t); p11: © Getty images/Jordan Mansfield; p12: © Getty images/Paul Ellis/AFP (l), © Stefan Chabluk (r); p13: © Getty images/Saeed Khan (l), © Getty images/ishara S. Kodikara/AFP (r); p14: © Getty images/Gareth Copley; p15: © Getty images/Stu Forster (l), © Getty images/Anesh Debiky/AFP (r); p16: © Getty images/ Manjunath Kiran/AFP; p17: © Getty images/William West/AFP (l), © Getty images/Bradley Kanaris (br), © Getty images/ian Kington/AFP (tr); p18: © Getty images/Brett Hemmings (r), © Getty images/Emmanuel Dunand/AFP (l); p19: © Getty images/Patrick Eagar (b), © Getty images/Paul Kane (t); p20: © Getty images; p21: © Getty images/Alexander Joe/AFP (l), © Getty images/Jewel Samad/AFP (br), © Getty images/Andrew Yates (tr); p22: © Getty images/Harry Engels (b); p23: © Getty images/Manjunath Kiran/AFP (l), © Getty images/Matthew Lewis, © Getty images/Marwan Naamani/AFP; p24: © Getty images/Scott Barbour (b), © iDi via Getty images/Pal Pillai-iDi (t); p25: © Getty images/Gareth Copley (t), © Getty images/Joel Ford (m), © Getty images/Alexander Joe/AFP (b); p26 © Getty images/Stu Forster (t, m, b); p27 © Getty images/David Rogers (tl), © Getty images/Paul Ellis/AFP, © Getty images/Stu Forster (b); p28 © Getty images/Mark Kolbe; p29: © Stefan Chalbuk (l), Getty images/Bob Thomas/Popperfoto (r); p30: © Getty images/Scott Barbour (t), © iCC via Getty images/Matthew Lewis-iCC; p31: © Getty images/Hagen Hopkins; p32: © Getty images/Randy Brooks. All graphic elements are courtesy of Shutterstock.com.

The website addresses (URLs) included in this book were valid at the time of going to press. However, it is possible that contents or addresses may have changed since the publication of this book. No responsibility for any such changes can be accepted by either the author or the Publisher.

Wayland is a division of Hachette Children's Books, an Hachette UK company.
www.hachette.co.uk

Contents

21st-century game   4

All the gear   6

Meet the umpires   8

Howzat!   10

Batting   12

Making runs   14

All the shots   16

Bowling   18

Seam and swing   20

In a spin   22

Fielding   24

Keeping wicket   26

Captaincy and tactics   28

Glossary   30

Further information   31

Index   32

3

21st-century game

Cricket is a sport that pitches two teams, usually of eleven players, against each other in a titanic battle of skill, speed, reactions and tactics. Its old reputation as a slow, gentle sport is no more. Cricket can be fast, furious, colourful and exciting with large crowds roaring on their own team.

Action athletes

Professional cricketers are top-level athletes. Some, like South African paceman Dale Steyn, are able to bowl the ball at speeds of over 150km/h. Others, like Pakistan's Shahid Afridi, can strike a cricket ball more than 90m through the air with their bats, whilst fielders regularly leap and dive to stop the ball or take a catch. It's not all pace and power, though. Cricket is also big on more subtle skills such as clever spin bowling and cheeky flick and glance shots.

Intimidating Australian fast bowler Mitchell Johnson bowls a pacy delivery against England in the 5th Ashes Test in 2014. Johnson took 37 wickets in the series.

BIG RUNS

Scoring 100 runs in a single innings is called a century and is a milestone batsmen love to reach. Some players have scored a lot more. Here are the three highest scores in first class cricket:

501	Brian Lara	Warwickshire v Durham, 1994
499	Hanif Mohammad	Karachi v Bahawalpur, 1959
452	Donald Bradman	New South Wales v Queensland, 1929

The 'Little Master' first played for India when he was 15 years old and has become the leading batsman of the past 50 years. Tendulkar has scored more Test match runs (15,291) than any other player and a record 18,426 runs in One Day Internationals (ODIs). This included the first ever ODI double century (200 or more runs in an innings). He also took 200 wickets as a bowler in Tests and ODIs. Worshipped throughout India, Tendulkar retired in 2013 after his 200th Test Match.

SACHIN TENDULKAR

The New Zealand team appeal to the umpire during a 2014 Test Match as they think Indian batsman Virat Kohli is out.

Innings

Each team takes a turn to bat, known as their innings. Pairs of batsmen bat at one time, and try to score runs. The opposing team, known as the fielding side, try both to stop runs being scored and to get the batsmen out. When a batsman is out they lose their wicket, leave the pitch and a teammate takes their place. When ten batsmen are out, a team's innings ends and the other team takes their turn to bat. Some forms of cricket are based on a set number of overs (six balls are bowled per over) that each team face, trying to score the most runs.

All the gear

A cricketer's clothing consists of long trousers, a shirt and cricket boots fitted with short spikes that grip the ground and help cricketers to sprint. In cooler conditions, a player may wear a jumper or sleeveless sweater. In Test matches and first class cricket such as the County Championship in the UK, clothing is white, but bright, coloured kits are worn in one-day cricket and Twenty20 (T20) competitions.

Protective clothing

Batsmen and wicketkeepers wear plenty of protection and, with a ball speeding towards them at over 100km/h, who can blame them! Batsmen wear padded gloves and large pads that protect their lower legs. Many wear additional protection including pads on their thighs and a forearm guard on their leading (front) arm when batting. In the past, top players such as Sir Vivian Richards would face fast bowling with no head or face protection, but today, almost all players wear a helmet, often with a visor to protect their face.

Wicketkeepers wear pads like a batsman but theirs are shorter and lighter in weight, making them easier to move around in. A keeper's gloves have protection for the ends of the fingers and webbed areas between the thumb and first finger.

Bat and ball

Cricket bats are made of wood, with a long handle covered in a rubber grip. They can weigh up to 1.4kg but must not be more than 96.5cm long and 10.8cm wide. A cricket ball is made of layers of cork and tightly wound string covered in a leather case, which is stitched to form the ball's seam. Cricket balls were once always dyed red but today many matches, such as ODIs and T20s, use white balls because they show up better against the players' coloured clothing.

England opening batsman Michael Carberry wore a new high-tech helmet in the 2013/14 Ashes Test matches in Australia. It inflates with air when a button is pushed so it fits tightly onto the head and cushions it if the ball hits.

India's Yuvraj Singh hits an attacking shot with South African wicketkeeper Quinton de Kock behind the stumps. Both men are wearing protective helmets with a metal grille to prevent facial injuries.

The long, flat face of a cricket bat is called the blade. Batsmen aim to strike the ball firmly in the middle of the bat.

Dennis Lillee caused a big argument in a 1979 Test match when he began batting with a bat made of aluminium. The laws of cricket were altered after this to insist on bats being made of wood.

Other ball colours have been experimented with. In 2009, a pink ball was used in an international match for the first time when England beat Australia by one run in a women's ODI.

Meet the umpires

Cricket has many rules known as laws. These are applied by two officials called umpires. One stands behind the stumps at the bowler's end and the other stands in a position called square leg (see p29). They switch positions after each over. In bigger games, a third umpire sits in the cricket ground, has access to TV footage and can be asked to rule on close decisions such as run-outs.

Lots of jobs

Umpires have to judge a whole range of things every ball, including did the bowler bowl a fair delivery, was a run scored and was the batsman out (see pp10-11)? Umpires also warn players about any behaviour that breaks the laws of the game, and check on the state of the ball and the weather conditions. They may take the teams off the field if the light is not good enough for the batsmen to play, or if rain falls.

Australian umpire Bruce Oxenford watches closely as Sri Lanka's Nuwan Pradeep comes in to bowl. The umpire must make split-second decisions over runs, whether a bowler has infringed or whether a batsman is out.

Light-up bails were first used in Australia's Big Bash T20 competition. Small LED lights inside each bail start flashing brightly if the bails are dislodged from the stumps – perfect for night games.

Six balls an over

Amongst the umpires' many jobs is counting the number of balls bowled. There are six balls in a regular over, but if the umpire decides that a bowler has bowled a wide or a no ball (see p19), the ball has to be re-bowled.

MOST ODI MATCHES UMPIRED		
209	Rudi Koertzen	South Africa
189	Billy Bowden	New Zealand
181	Steve Bucknor	Jamaica
174	Daryl Harper	Australia
174	Simon Taufel	Australia

Out Leg-bye No ball Bye

Boundary 6 Boundary 4 Wide Disregard last signal

Umpires communicate their signals to the scorers, teams and fans using a range of signals. These are some of the most common.

Bails •••••••••
Stumps •••••••••

Whitewashed pitch markings are called creases. The popping crease is 1.22m ahead of the bowling crease which is in line with the stumps.

• Popping crease

Pitching up

The cricket pitch sits in the middle of a cricket ground. It's a 20.12m-long, 3.05m-wide strip of carefully prepared ground with a set of wickets at each end. These are made of three 71.1cm-tall stumps topped by two pieces of wood called bails. Together, the stumps and bails are known as the wicket. The ground that makes up every pitch behaves slightly differently, which is one of the appeals of cricket. Some pitches are hard and very bouncy, whilst others are softer and slower or develop small cracks which mean that if the ball hits them, it may bounce up at an unexpected angle.

Howzat!

Watch a cricket game for long enough and you'll hear, "Howzat!" It's the bowler and his teammates appealing to the umpire. They think the other team's batsman is out and are asking the umpire for a decision. Some decisions are simple. If the ball is bowled, hits the stumps and topples one or both of the bails off the top of them, then the batsman is out, bowled. But there are a further nine ways a batsman can be out, including stumping (see p27).

(see p27)

Rana Naveed takes a diving catch to dismiss Rob Quiney during the Twenty20 Big Bash in Australia.

Catches

Catches win matches and being caught is the most common dismissal (way of being out) in many forms of cricket. A player is out, caught, if the ball hits the bat, or the batsman's glove when it's in contact with the bat, and is caught before it touches the ground. Some catches are made when the ball hits the bat, then the pads or foot of a fielder, and balloons up into the air.

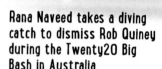

An umpire must judge where the ball pitches, and whether it would have gone on to hit the stumps in order to give a batsman out, LBW.

In a 2009 County Championship game, fielder Jonathan Trott turned away as batsman Ed Joyce hit the ball at him – only to find it had flown into his trouser pocket! Joyce was given out, caught by Trott.

Leg before wicket

One of the most complicated laws in cricket, LBWs keep TV and radio commentators buzzing with chat, opinion and lots of action replays. The basic rule is that if the ball has pitched in line with the stumps (the red arrow) and would have gone on to hit them but is stopped by the player's pads or body, then the player may be given out LBW. If the ball pitches outside leg stump (the purple arrow), you cannot be out LBW, even if the ball would have gone on to hit the stumps.

Run-outs

Run-outs occur when a batsman doesn't get their bat, or part of their body, touching the ground past the popping crease to complete a run before the fielding side knock the bails off with the ball. Fielders either aim for the stumps directly or throw the ball to a teammate nearer the stumps who completes the run-out.

OTHER WAYS TO BE OUT
There are five less common ways a batsman can be out:

- Timed out – a batsman takes too long to appear on the field in time.
- Obstructing the field – the batsman stops a fielder from making a catch or run-out.
- Hitting the ball twice – the batsman's bat hits the ball twice in the same delivery.
- Handled ball – the batsman uses his or her hands to stop the ball hitting the stumps.
- Hit wicket – when the batsman treads on or falls onto the stumps or their bat hits the stumps.

No doubts about this wicket falling as Alex Blake's stumps are broken by a ball bowled by Gareth Batty during a T20 Blast match between Kent Spitfires and Surrey.

11

Kevin Pietersen's helmet fell off and landed on the stumps whilst he batted against the West Indies in 2007, making him one of the most recent players to be out, hit wicket.

Batting

Every player in a team might get a chance to bat so even tailenders – players who are in the side for their bowling not their batting – practise hard to improve their batting so they can stay in and make runs. Stuart Broad, for example, was the ninth batsman in during England's 2010 Test match versus Pakistan, but he still managed to score an incredible 169 runs in his innings.

Stance

Batsmen need to be balanced and ready for the ball as it is bowled. They grip their bat with both hands and balance their weight on the balls of their feet so they can quickly rock back or move forward, depending on the shot they play. Their front shoulder points down the pitch and their eyes focus on the ball as it leaves the bowler's hand.

AGAR AMAZES
Ashton Agar made a surprise debut for Australia in 2013 in a Test match versus England. The 19 year old became the first Australian spin bowler to take a wicket as a teenager, but it was with the bat that he astonished spectators. Playing his first ever Test innings as the last batsman in, few thought he would last for long. But Agar scored 98 runs - the most by a number 11 Test batsman, ever.

England captain Alistair Cook practises his batting in the nets. He lifts his bat back as the ball is bowled and decides which shot to play.

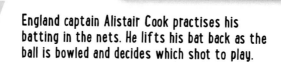

Yorker
Full pitched

Good length

Short pitched

Bouncer

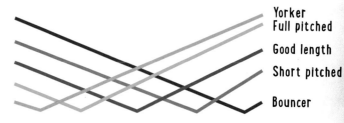

How far the ball lands down the pitch often determines how high the ball will rise towards the batsman. These are typical paths of balls bowled by a fast or medium-fast bowler.

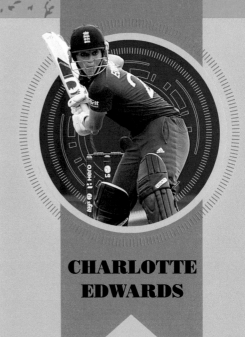

HIGHEST SCORES IN ODIs

These matches are 50 overs (300 balls) per team, so all of the following teams scored very quickly at more than a run per ball.

443	for 9	Sri Lanka v Netherlands, 2006
438	for 9	South Africa v Australia, 2006
434	for 4	Australia v South Africa, 2006
418	for 5	South Africa v Zimbabwe, 2006
418	for 5	India v West Indies, 2011

CHARLOTTE EDWARDS

Gary Ballance plays a forward defensive shot on England's 2013/14 tour of Australia. His bat and front pad are angled together to form a barrier to stop the ball.

A star batter in all forms of the game, Edwards played her first match for England at the age of 16. The day before her 18th birthday, she scored 173 not out in a World Cup match against Ireland and has hit over 5,400 runs in ODIs. She has also scored four centuries in Test cricket. In 2014, she became the first female cricketer to score more than 2,000 runs in Twenty20 internationals.

13

Shot or not?

Batsmen sometimes let a ball pass them, or play a defensive shot to protect their wicket. On other occasions, they will strike the ball fiercely. They must try to select the right shot for each ball they face. This depends on the speed and type of bowler they are facing but also their judgement of where the ball will pitch. The batsman has to estimate the length of the ball (see diagram, left) as a sharp, short-pitched delivery has to be played differently to a fuller-length ball. They must also judge the line of the ball; whether it is towards their stumps, wide on the offside or on a legside line. All of these judgements have to be made in a fraction of a second.

Making runs

Batting takes patience, concentration and a good eye for a chance to score a run. Once the ball is struck, the batsman and his partner at the other end of the pitch have to make a decision. Can they make a run before the fielders retrieve the ball and throw to the stumps? Clear, definite calls between the two batsmen are vital as many run-outs occur when one player sets off for a run and the other stays still. To complete a run, both batsmen swap ends of the pitch, crossing in the middle. As they reach the popping crease, they must ground their bats. If the chance is on for a second run, they can set off again.

14

Batsmen try to form partnerships with a teammate, scoring as many runs together as possible. The world record partnership is held by Sri Lankan pair Kumar Sangakkara and Mahela Jayawardene. In a 2006 Test match against South Africa, they scored a staggering 624 runs together in an innings.

Sarah Taylor and Charlotte Edwards run between the wickets during the semi-final of the Women's World T20 in 2014.

Building an innings

Fours and sixes may excite crowds but sometimes, crucial runs are made by nudging the ball into gaps between fielders and running hard. When a good batsman is batting with a tailender, they may look to run a single near the end of the over so they are at the batting end come the next over. A batsman looks to pace his or her innings and may adjust how they play depending on new bowlers coming on or if their side loses a number of wickets suddenly.

This hard-hitting, aggressive batsman first made his name in T20 where, on his debut for Australia versus South Africa in 2009, he scored 89 runs off just 43 balls. He has since scored five T20 international 100s as well as eight 100s in Test Matches. His 100 against India in 2012 took just 69 balls, the fastest ever made by an opening batsman (one of the two batsmen that start a team's innings).

DAVID WARNER

Fours and sixes

The boundary is the edge of the cricket ground. A well-hit shot reaching the boundary scores four runs. If a fielder stops the ball but is touching the boundary as they do so, the umpire will still signal a four. If a batsman hits the ball high over the boundary without it touching the ground, the umpire will signal a six. India's Rohit Sharma scored 209 runs in a One Day International versus Australia in 2013, of which an incredible 144 were fours (12) and sixes (16). This is the most sixes ever hit in an ODI innings.

15

SIX SIXES

Only five players have hit six sixes in an over in professional cricket:

1968	Sir Garfield Sobers	Nottinghamshire v Glamorgan
1984	Ravi Shastri	Bombay v Baroda
2007	Herschelle Gibbs	South Africa v the Netherlands
2007	Yuvraj Singh	India v England
2013	Jordan Clark	Lancashire 2nd XI v Yorkshire 2nd XI

India's Rohit Sharma pulls a ball for six during a 2014 ODI against India. Sharma has struck 66 sixes and 279 fours in One Day Internationals.

All the shots

Batsmen work for hour after hour in cricket nets to rehearse and improve the different shots they can play. The more shots they can master, the more tools they have to deal with the opposing team's bowling and the more ways they can find to score runs.

Different strokes

Drives are shots played back down the ground, either side of the stumps at the far end. The batsman times the shot and gets their bat angled slightly forward at the handle to keep the ball down, so as not to give away a catching chance. A pull shot is played to a ball that reaches the batsman at around waist height. The batsman looks to hit it powerfully through the leg side. A hook shot is similar but riskier as it's played to a ball coming at between chest and head height.

In recent years, batsmen have developed several new shots to score runs in places regular shots can't reach. One of the most striking is the 'Dilscoop', named after Sri Lanka's Tillakaratne Dilshan. He pioneered this high-risk shot where the bat is pointed straight down the pitch and then tilted upwards to scoop the ball over the batsman and wicketkeeper's heads.

QUICK CENTURIES
Here are the five fastest 100s scored by batsmen in One Day Internationals:

Balls	Player	Country	Year
36	Corey Anderson	New Zealand	2014
37	Shahid Afridi	Pakistan	1996
44	Mark Boucher	South Africa	2006
45	Brian Lara	West Indies	1999
45	Shahid Afridi	Pakistan	2005

Ian Bell puts his wide range of shots to good use, defending and accumulating runs when the bowling is tough, and hitting more aggressive shots when on the attack. Bell has scored 21 centuries for England in Test matches, including a high score of 235 against India. In 2013, he scored three centuries in four matches against Australia and was voted Player of the Series.

IAN BELL

England's Joe Root plays a straight drive with the full face of the bat to punch the ball straight back the ground.

Placement and power

Some shots are all about timing and skill, rather than power. A leg glance, for instance, sees a batsman deflect a ball heading down the leg side, away from the reach of the wicketkeeper. If well timed and directed, this deceptively gentle stroke can result in the ball reaching the boundary and four runs being scored. A sweep shot sees a player get low, often on one knee, and paddle the ball round the corner behind them.

James Hopes gets down on one knee to sweep the ball down the leg side during a 2013 Sheffield Shield match.

Bowling

Bowlers bowl an over from one end of the pitch. Each ball they bowl is known as a delivery. A bowler is often brought on for a number of overs, intent on both taking wickets and giving away as few runs as possible. Most cricket teams go into a match with three, four or five specialist bowlers, whilst several more members of the team may get a chance to bowl as well.

Bowling a delivery

Every bowler has a slightly different bowling action but all start with a run up to the wicket. Approaching the stumps, they take a bound through the air, turning their body sideways as they leap. As they land, they bring their arm up and over their head in a big circle, releasing the ball when their hand is at its highest to send it flying down the pitch.

England spin bowler Moeen Ali bowls during a 2014 ODI against the West Indies.

Australia's Ellyse Perry is coiled perfectly as she takes her delivery leap before bowling the ball against England in a 2014 ODI in Hobart, Australia.

ELLYSE PERRY

Perry made her debuts for both the Australian women's cricket and women's football teams at the age of 16. An all-rounder (a player picked for their batting and bowling), Perry is a fast-medium bowler who took 5 wickets for just 19 runs against India in a 2012 ODI. At the age of 23, she has already taken 100 wickets in Tests and ODIs as well as a further 56 wickets in women's T20 internationals.

Wides and no balls

Bowlers need to be accurate and avoid bowling wides and no balls. A wide occurs if the umpire believes the ball was bowled too wide or too high for the batsman to reach. No balls occur for many reasons but the most common are when the bowler's front foot oversteps the popping crease as they release the ball. The batsman cannot be bowled, caught or out LBW from a wide or no ball but one run is added to the batting team's score and the ball is bowled again. In some limited-over games, two runs are added for a no ball.

Pakistan bowler Mohammad Sami ended up bowling an over containing 17 balls in a 2004 ODI versus Bangladesh. Sami struggled to bowl the ball straight and bowled seven wides and four no balls in one over!

19

MOST WICKETS TAKEN BY ENGLAND ODI BOWLERS	
Jimmy Anderson	255
Darren Gough	234
Andrew Flintoff	168
Stuart Broad	168
Ian Botham	145

Australian pace bowler Glenn McGrath bowls with a perfect high-arm release of the ball.

Seam and swing

Fast bowlers send the ball hurtling down the pitch towards the batsman. Some, like Australia's Mitchell Johnson, rely on extreme pace and bounce to unsettle the batsman and may bowl bouncers – deliveries that rear up off the pitch at the batsman's chest and head. Others look to move the ball through the air or off the pitch to get wickets.

The fastest ball bowled is believed to have been by Shoaib Akhtar of Pakistan at the 2003 World Cup. England's Nick Knight was the batsman who had to face the delivery, which was measured at 161.3km/h – faster than many cars!

This grip is for a seam bowler bowling a slower ball. The fingers are spaced either side of the seam to offer control as the ball is released.

Seam bowling

Seam bowlers grip the ball seam up, with the seam vertical. They aim for the ball to land on the seam and change direction off the pitch as a result. Great seam bowlers like Dale Steyn bowl fast and accurately, landing each ball precisely where they aim it, to put pressure on the batsman. They may vary their line (how wide of the stumps they aim the ball) and the length of each delivery (how far down the pitch they aim the ball to land) in order to keep the batsman uncertain.

LEADING WICKET TAKERS

Here are the leading Test-wicket-taking swing and seam bowlers playing today, along with their bowling average (the number of runs scored off their deliveries divided by the number of wickets they've taken).

Player	Wickets	Average
Dale Steyn	383	22.56
Jimmy Anderson	380	29.72
Zaheer Khan	311	32.94
Mitchell Johnson	264	27.42
Stuart Broad	264	29.90

Swing bowling

Some bowlers, such as Jimmy Anderson and Zaheer Khan, are able to make the ball swing in the air into or away from the batsman after it leaves their hand. This can trick the batsman into playing the wrong shot before the ball reaches them. Keeping one side of the ball polished and shiny aids swing bowling, as does a cloudy, overcast day.

Dale Steyn braces his body and front leg as he whips his bowling arm over. The South African paceman is a devastating swing and seam bowler.

JIMMY ANDERSON

Jimmy Anderson is England's star pace bowler. Accurate and relentless, Anderson can often get the ball to swing fiercely through the air, posing real problems to batsmen. In 2013, he became the fourth English bowler to take 300 Test wickets. In the same year, he became the latest bowler to bowl through an entire innings without rest when he destroyed New Zealand in a Test match by taking 7 wickets for 44 runs.

Stuart Broad brings his arm over to bowl a fast delivery. Broad uses his 1.96m height to send the ball down sharply to the opposing batsman.

In a spin

Spin bowlers bowl more slowly than fast bowlers but have different weapons besides sheer pace to beat batsmen. The way they grip and release the ball makes it spin as it travels through the air. As the ball lands, this spin can cause it to deviate sideways, sometimes sharply enough to get past a batsman.

A good grip for bowling off-spin sees the middle joints of the first and middle finger resting on the ball's seam.

England spinner Holly Colvin flicks her wrist and fingers to put spin on the ball as she releases it. The left arm spinner has taken over 170 wickets for England.

Off spin and leg spin

Off-spin bowlers put spin on the ball with their first two fingers so that when bowling to a right-handed batsman the ball pitches from the off side to the leg side. This is called an off break. Leg spinners use a powerful snap of the wrist to generate spin on the ball so that it deviates in the opposite direction to an off break. Shane Warne was the greatest ever leg spinner, taking 708 wickets in Tests and a further 293 in ODIs.

When the pitch suits spin, a talented spin bowler can dominate the opposition. In a 1956 Test match, England off-spin bowler Jim Laker took nine wickets in the first innings and all 10 Australian wickets in the second innings, finishing the match with 19 for 90 runs.

This Sri Lankan magician is the only player to have taken 10 wickets in a match against all the leading Test-match-playing nations. In a long career, Muralitharan bowled over 62,000 balls in Tests and ODIs and is the all-time leading wicket taker in both forms of the game, with 534 ODI wickets and a staggering 800 Test wickets.

Sri Lankan spin maestro Muttiah Muralitharan prepares to bowl in an IPL T20 match for his side, Royal Challengers Bangalore.

MUTTIAH MURALITHARAN

Spin variations

Successful spin bowlers develop different types of delivery to keep the batsman guessing. Some off-spinners, such as Pakistan's Saeed Ajmal, are able to bowl a ball called the doosra, which spins off the pitch in the opposite direction to an off break. Some spinners like to bowl an 'arm ball' which looks like it will spin but instead goes straight on when it lands on the pitch. Spinners may also vary the amount of flight they give the ball (how looped or flat the ball travels out of the hand) with the aim of tricking the batsman into playing the wrong shot.

Saeed Ajmal bowls in a T20 against Sri Lanka. Ajmal's control and use of the doosra has seen him take over 400 international wickets.

MUTTIAH'S 800 TEST WICKETS BY OPPOSING TEAM

Wickets	Opponents	Matches
112	England	16
105	India	22
104	South Africa	15
89	Bangladesh	11
87	Zimbabwe	14
82	New Zealand	14
82	West Indies	12
80	Pakistan	16
59	Australia	13

Fielding

Top teams in T20s and other forms of cricket are packed with fielding demons – great athletes who train hard and often so that their skills are sharp. Accurate fielding not only stops runs, it can also lead to wickets through run-outs and catches. Stopping runs can also mount pressure on batsmen, forcing them into a mistake.

Stopping runs

Fielders stay alert and focus on the ball as it's bowled, because it may come thundering towards them a second later. A fielder's first aim is to get to the ball, to stop it going past them if they can, or to chase it down as quickly as possible. Fumbling the ball or slowness in getting to the ball can lead to opponents stealing an extra run or two.

MOST CAREER CATCHES IN TEST MATCHES		
210	Rahul Dravid	India
205	Mahela Jayawardene	Sri Lanka
200	Jacques Kallis	South Africa
196	Ricky Ponting	Australia
181	Mark Waugh	Australia

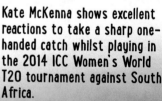

Kate McKenna shows excellent reactions to take a sharp one-handed catch whilst playing in the 2014 ICC Women's World T20 tournament against South Africa.

Dwayne Bravo keeps his eyes on the ball as he flies through the air to take a brilliant diving catch for the West Indies against Australia in the ICC World Twenty20 competition.

Ian Bell is surrounded by Australian close fielders waiting to pounce on a loose shot to make a catch during the 2013/14 Ashes Series.

Throwing in

Once retrieved, the ball must be thrown back as fast and accurately as possible to a teammate who has got close to the stumps – a technique known as backing up. A poor throw can see the ball go loose again and the batsmen can then choose to carry on running. These extra runs are known as overthrows and can be expensive. In a 2008 Test match, four overthrows by New Zealand fielders meant that Australia scored eight runs off a single ball!

Catch it!

Catches come to fielders at all different speeds, heights and angles. Some call for lightning reactions and spectacular dives to get near the ball. Others see the fielder stay in position, keep their nerve and watch the ball right into their hands. As the ball arrives, a catcher wraps their hands around it and tries to cushion the ball's impact by allowing their hands and arms to withdraw into their body.

New Zealander Jono Boult throws the ball back hard and flat to reach his wicketkeeper.

Australian fast bowler Patrick Cummins slides along the ground to stop the ball reaching the boundary during a Test match versus South Africa.

25

Keeping wicket

Wicketkeepers are a cricket team's heartbeat. For over after over, they have to gather the ball cleanly into their gloves after it has been bowled, but always remain alert to making an acrobatic catch or a lightning-fast stumping chance. Theirs is a tough job and wicketkeepers need to be extremely fit, flexible and possess epic powers of concentration.

A keeper's duties

A wicketkeeper chooses how far behind the stumps they stand and will vary it depending on the speed of the bowler. As the ball is bowled, they rise from a crouched position, staying on the balls of their feet ready to take a step to one side, leap high, or dive sharply to catch the ball. They will have to keep wicket to 300 or more balls in an ODI game and hundreds more in a Test match, so fitness and stamina are crucial. Modern keepers such as India's M.S. Dhoni and England's Jos Buttler and Sarah Taylor are also expected to be excellent batsmen.

South Africa's Mark Boucher is alert to the ball coming in to him and watches it right into his hands.

ODI WICKETKEEPERS

Two players lead the ODI rankings for catches and stumpings taken as wicketkeeper:

Player	Nationality	Catches	Stumpings
Kumar Sangakkara	Sri Lanka	359	89
M.S. Dhoni	India	226	83

MOST WICKETKEEPER DISMISSALS IN A TEST MATCH

11	Jack Russell	England v South Africa, 1995
11	A.B. de Villiers	South Africa v Pakistan, 2013
10	Bob Taylor	England v India, 1980
10	Adam Gilchrist	Australia v New Zealand, 2000

Warwickshire keeper Richard Johnson takes a smart diving catch, getting both gloves around the ball before he hits the ground.

Stumped!

When a batsman moves down the pitch to hit the ball, the wicketkeeper stays alert for a stumping chance. If the batsman misses the ball, the keeper tries to gather it quickly and knock the bails off the stumps. If the batsman has not got their foot or bat on the ground past the popping crease in time, then the umpire will give the batsman out, stumped. Batsmen cannot be stumped off a no ball, but they can be stumped off a wide.

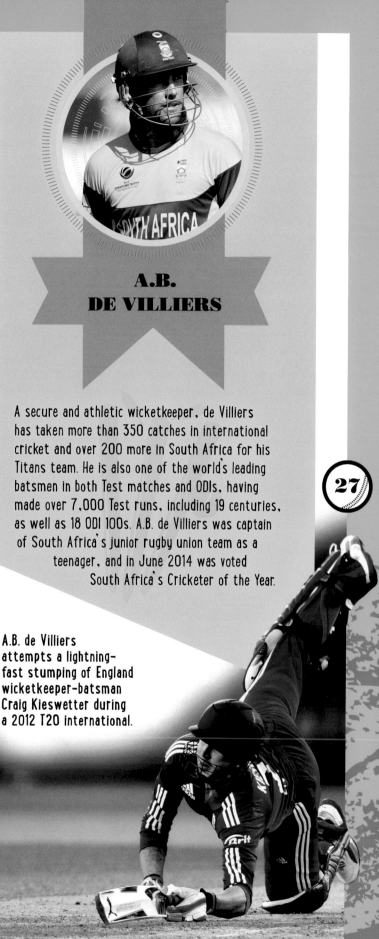

A.B. DE VILLIERS

A secure and athletic wicketkeeper, de Villiers has taken more than 350 catches in international cricket and over 200 more in South Africa for his Titans team. He is also one of the world's leading batsmen in both Test matches and ODIs, having made over 7,000 Test runs, including 19 centuries, as well as 18 ODI 100s. A.B. de Villiers was captain of South Africa's junior rugby union team as a teenager, and in June 2014 was voted South Africa's Cricketer of the Year.

A.B. de Villiers attempts a lightning-fast stumping of England wicketkeeper-batsman Craig Kieswetter during a 2012 T20 international.

Captaincy and tactics

A captain manages a team's players and tactics. Teams can play in many different ways and their tactics may change a number of times during the same match. A fielding team, for example, may play defensively, trying to stop their opponents scoring runs, but as soon as they get several wickets, they may go more on the attack and try to bowl the opposing team out.

The captain

Captains toss a coin before the game starts, and the winner decides whether their team will bat or bowl first. They make that decision based on the state of the weather and pitch, as well as their own team's strengths and the opposition's weaknesses. Captains also have to decide the order in which their players go in to bat. Whilst fielding, a captain constantly considers how the game is going, and picks who bowls, when and for how many overs.

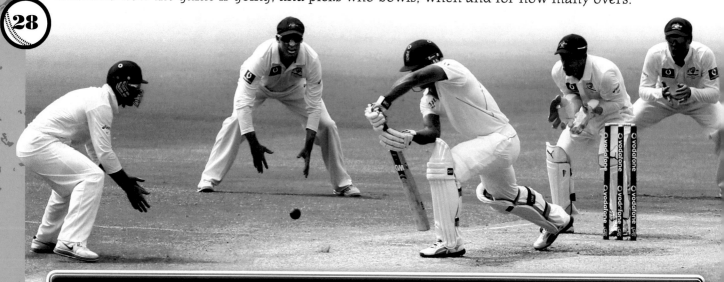

LONGEST WINNING RUN IN TEST MATCHES, ODIS AND T20 INTERNATIONALS		
20	Australia	2003
16	Australia	2000-01
16	Australia	2006-07
14	Pakistan	1990
14	Pakistan	2011-12

MOST TEST MATCHES AS CAPTAIN		
109	Graeme Smith	South Africa, 2003-14
93	Allan Border	Australia, 1984-94
80	Stephen Fleming	New Zealand, 1997-2006
77	Ricky Ponting	Australia, 2004-10
74	Clive Lloyd	West Indies, 1974-1985

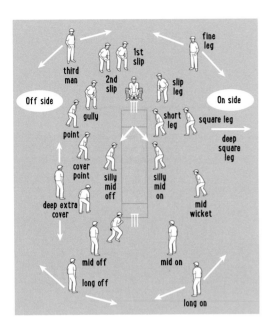

The T20, ODI and Test captain of India, Mahendra Singh Dhoni is an attacking batsman and wicketkeeper, always at the centre of the action. Dhoni first led India to success in the 2007 T20 World Cup and four years later captained his side to win the 2011 ODI World Cup, hitting 91 runs in the final versus Sri Lanka. His clever captaincy also helped India become the number-one-ranked Test nation for 18 months straight.

MAHENDRA SINGH DHONI

There are dozens of different fielding positions and captains choose and instruct their teammates where to stand. These are some of the most common.

Australia's fielders crowd round South African batsman Faf du Plessis as Australian captain Michael Clark presses for a victory. Du Plessis managed to score 110 to help draw the match.

In the field

Captains decide where to place their team's fielders. This will depend on the bowler and also the match situation. A defensive field is one where the fielders are placed around the ground to stop runs, whilst an attacking field usually has lots of fielders close to the batsman hoping to take a catch. Canny captains are skilled at changing tactics and making small, subtle shifts in the position of their fielders even in between balls of the same over.

Glossary

All-rounder A player capable of both bowling and batting well.

Ashes A Test match series between England and Australia, played roughly every two years.

Average (batting) The number of runs scored in a career or season divided by the number of innings in which the batsman was out.

Average (bowling) The number of runs scored off a bowler's overs divided by the number of wickets he or she has taken.

Bails The wooden rods placed on top of the stumps to form a wicket.

Boundary The edge of a cricket field and the name given to a batsman hitting the ball over it to score a four or six.

Bye A run scored when the batsman does not touch the ball with his or her bat or body.

Century 100 or more runs scored by an individual batsman.

Delivery The word used to describe a ball bowled at the batsman by a bowler.

Flight The path of the ball through the air when it is bowled.

LBW Short for Leg Before Wicket, it is one of the ways a batsman can be out.

Leg side The area of pitch behind the batsman's legs when he or she faces the ball.

Length Where the ball pitches down the wicket. A full length is closer to the batsman than a good length or short ball.

ODIs Short for One Day Internationals – 50 overs-per-side matches played between national teams.

Off side The side of the pitch that is to a batsman's right (if right-handed), or left (if left-handed).

Opening batsman A player who bats at the very start of his or her team's innings.

Over A series of six legal deliveries bowled by a bowler from one end of the pitch.

Partnership The number of runs scored by a pair of batsmen when they bat together.

Test match The ultimate form of cricket, a Test match is played over five days, with two innings per side.

Twenty20 A form of the game where each side bats a maximum of 20 overs each.

Umpires The officials who control a cricket match and make key decisions on whether a player is out or not and whether runs have been scored.

Wide A ball that bounces so high or lands so wide of the stumps that it is very hard for a batsman to reach it.

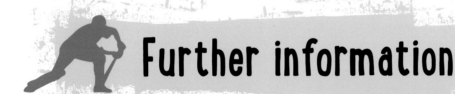

Further information

Inside Sport: Cricket by Clive Gifford (Wayland, 2014). A comprehensive look at the sport of cricket around the world.

Sporting Skills: Cricket by Clive Gifford (Wayland, 2014). Learn how to perfect the skills, tactics and theory of cricket.

http://www.espncricinfo.com
A feature- and stat-packed website with profiles on all leading players and thousands of cricket records.

http://www.bbc.co.uk/sport/0/cricket/womens
These BBC webpages cover women's cricket with fixtures, results and links to other sites.

http://www.ecb.co.uk/development/get-into-cricket
Ways of getting into cricket in the UK can be found at these webpages run by the English Cricket Board (ECB).

Index

Afridi, Shahid 4, 16
Agar, Ashton 12
Anderson, Jimmy 19, 20, 21
Ashes, the 4, 7, 25, 30
Australia 4, 7, 8, 9, 10, 13, 15, 17, 18, 19, 20, 22, 23, 24, 25, 26, 28, 29

bails 9, 10, 11, 27, 30
balls 4, 5, 6, 7, 8, 9, 10, 11, 12, 13, 14, 15, 16, 17, 18, 19, 20, 21, 22, 23, 24, 25, 26, 27
  colour 7
Bangladesh 19, 23
bats 4, 7, 10, 11, 12, 13, 14, 16, 17, 27
batsmen & batting 4, 5, 6, 7, 8, 10, 11, 12-17, 19, 20, 21, 22, 23, 24, 26, 27, 28, 29
  out 5, 8, 9, 10, 11, 19, 27, 28
  shots 7, 12, 13, 15, 16-17, 21, 25
Bell, Ian 17, 25
Boucher, Mark 16, 26
bowlers & bowling 4, 5, 8, 9, 10, 11, 12, 16, 17, 18-23, 25, 26, 28, 29
  fast 4, 6, 12, 20, 21, 22, 25
  no ball 9, 19, 27
  seam 20, 21
  spin 4, 12, 18, 22-23
  swing 20, 21
  wide 9, 13, 19, 27, 31
Broad, Stuart 12, 19, 20, 21
Buttler, Jos 26

captains 12, 28-29
Carberry, Michael 7
catches 4, 10, 11, 16, 19, 24, 25, 26, 27, 29
clothing 6, 7
creases 9, 11, 14, 19, 27

de Villiers, A.B. 26, 27
Dhoni, Mahendra Singh 26, 29

Dilshan, Tillakaratne 16

Edwards, Charlotte 13, 14
England 7, 12, 13, 17, 18, 19, 21, 22, 23, 26, 27

fielders & fielding 4, 5, 10, 11, 14, 15, 24-27, 28
  overthrows 25
  positions 8, 29

India 5, 7, 13, 15, 17, 23, 24, 26, 29
innings 4, 5, 12, 14, 15, 21, 22

Jamaica 9
Jayawardene, Mahela 14, 24
Johnson, Mitchell 4, 20
Joyce, Ed 10

Khan, Zaheer 21

Laker, Jim 22
Lara, Brian 4, 16
laws 8, 10
leg before wicket (LBW) 10, 19, 30
Lillee, Dennis 7

Muralitharan, Muttiah 23

nets 12, 16
New Zealand 5, 9, 16, 21, 23, 25, 26, 28

One Day Internationals (ODIs) 5, 6, 7, 9, 13, 15, 16, 18, 19, 23, 26, 27, 28, 29, 31
overs 5, 8, 9, 13, 14, 18, 19, 26, 29, 31

pads 6, 10, 13
Pakistan 4, 16, 19, 23, 26, 28
Perry, Ellyse 18, 19
Pietersen, Kevin 11
pitching 10, 13
Ponting, Ricky 24, 28

Richards, Sir Vivian 6
run-outs 8, 11, 14, 24
runs 4, 5, 8, 11, 12, 13, 14-15, 16, 17, 18, 19, 20, 21, 22, 24, 25, 27, 28, 29
  centuries 4, 5, 12, 13, 15, 16, 17, 27, 29, 30
  fours 14, 15, 17
  sixes 14, 15

Sami, Mohammad 19
Sangakkara, Kumar 14, 26
South Africa 4, 7, 9, 13, 15, 16, 21, 23, 24, 25, 26, 27, 29
Sri Lanka 8, 13, 14, 16, 23, 24, 29
Steyn, Dale 4, 20
stumping 10, 26, 27
stumps 7, 8, 9, 10, 11, 13, 14, 16, 18, 20, 25, 26, 27

tailenders 12, 14
Taylor, Sarah 14, 26
Tendulkar, Sachin 5
Test matches 4, 5, 6, 7, 12, 13, 14, 15, 17, 20, 21, 22, 23, 25, 26, 27, 28, 29, 31
Trott, Jonathan 10
Twenty20 (T20) 6, 7, 9, 10, 11, 13, 14, 15, 23, 24, 27, 28, 29, 31

umpires 5, 8-9, 10, 15, 19, 27

weather 8, 21, 28
West Indies 11, 13, 16, 18, 23, 24, 28
wicketkeepers 6, 7, 16, 17, 25, 26-27, 29
wickets 9, 11, 13, 14, 18
  taking 4, 5, 12, 18, 19, 20, 21, 22, 23, 24, 28
women's cricket 7, 13, 14, 18, 19, 22, 24, 26
World Cup 13, 29

Zimbabwe 23

32